Dear Parent,

Have you ever wondered, *How can I show my child that Jesus loves him? And how do I teach him to love Jesus back?* Maybe you didn't come from a family that modeled Christ. Or maybe you had Christian influences growing up, but you still feel like you're fumbling a bit. Maybe your family looks very different from those portrayed in storybooks. So what should a Christian family really look like?

As you read this book with your child, you'll get to know a lovable family who live out ten transforming qualities of a Christian family—qualities that lead children to develop a personal desire to know Jesus. If you want your children to love Jesus, just let them see you praying, worshiping, spending time listening to God, calling on God first when there's trouble, forgiving and accepting forgiveness, serving with kindness, loving enemies, studying God's Word, and having "church" with others and at home. If your children see you doing these things, they are far more likely to love Jesus themselves!

So cuddle up with your child, enjoy the story, and take time to talk together about the ways you see your own family living out these qualities. You'll probably find that being a Christian family is not so hard after all. In fact, I'll bet this happy, approachable family will reveal that you are doing far better than you realize!

Growing with you,
Jennie Bishop

Published by Standard Publishing, Cincinnati, Ohio
www.standardpub.com

Printed in China

Editorial and creative direction: Robin Stanley
Project editor: Laura Derico
Cover and interior design: Sandra Wimmer

0-7847-1988-8

13 12 11 10 09 08 07   9 8 7 6 5 4 3 2 1

Library of Congress Cataloging-in-Publication Data

Bishop, Jennie.
  Jesus must be really special / by Jennie Bishop ; illustrated by Amy
Wummer.
      p. cm.
  ISBN 0-7847-1988-8 (case bound)
  1. Jesus Christ--Person and offices--Juvenile literature. 2. God--Worship
and love--Juvenile literature. I. Wummer, Amy. II. Title.

BT203.B54 2007
249--dc22

                                    2006026580

Jesus Must Be
Really Special

by Jennie Bishop

illustrated by Amy Wummer

Standard®
PUBLISHING
Bringing The Word to Life

Cincinnati, Ohio

To Stan and Jaime:
May your children see Jesus in you!
—J.B.

In loving memory of Dad,
who never missed his bedtime prayers.
—A.W.

Jesus must be really special,
because my mom and dad love
him so much.

I mean, they **REALLY** love him. I've
been watching them, and I know!

If God had a phone, my mom and dad
would have it glued to their ears.

They talk to him all the time. (That's called praying.)

They pray at bedtime.

They pray in the park.

Sometimes they pray for people they don't even know!

Hey! They're praying for **ME!**

I know my mom and dad love Jesus, because they play lots of music about him. Mom says that listening to songs with Bible words is like eating good food—it makes you healthy in your heart.

But we don't just listen to Bible songs, we **sing** them too—**everywhere we go!**

My dad sings out loud to Jesus all the time—even in the bathroom! I hear him singing, "I love you, Lord!"—and he's not even embarrassed!

His heart must be **very** healthy.

Jesus must be really special, because at our house, he's the first person we think of when we need help.

When my cat, George, climbed too high, I was scared (and George was too)! Dad said we should ask Jesus for help right then and there, and so we did.

Wow! Jesus heard us praying and sent a very **cool** answer.

Thank you for helping us, Jesus!

George is thankful too—
I can tell!

One time a boy at school was calling us names and teasing. I didn't know why he was being so mean. He even made my friend cry. I was very upset.

When I told Mom about how I felt, she reminded me that Jesus said we should **love** our enemies. She said that maybe the boy was angry because he thought nobody cared about him.

Mom and I prayed, "Jesus, show us how to be kind to this boy so he knows you love him." After that, I didn't feel angry anymore . . . I felt sad.

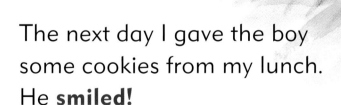

The next day I gave the boy some cookies from my lunch. He **smiled!**

(My mom sure knows a lot about Jesus' words!)

Jesus must be really special, because his book is my mom and dad's favorite.

It's called the **Bible.**

The words in there are very important. Dad has some of the important words colored with a bright green marker.
He says that the Bible helps him learn how to be like Jesus.

After dinner we play games and read stories. Sometimes we act like Bible people, and sometimes we just act goofy.

We **always** like to sing songs and have lots of **fun!**

One night I got to squeeze out a **whole** tube of toothpaste. Dad asked me to try to get the toothpaste back into the tube, but I couldn't. I just got my fingers all stickety-gooey!

"The things we say are like that," Dad said. "Once we say them, we can't put them back in our mouths. That's why Jesus wants us to be very careful to speak kindly to others."

I just can't stop thinking about that.
Every time I brush my teeth, I ask
Jesus to help me not get
stickety-gooey, unkind
words on **anybody.**

Jesus must be really special, because my
mom and dad are always thinking of ways
to show they love him.

We can show love to
Jesus by caring about
people, so my family
helps wash lots of cars
at church for **free!**

Some people ask us if we want money, but we don't
want any money. We just want them to know that
Jesus cares about them and so do **we!**

We can care about people **everywhere!**

My mom bakes yummy pies to take to the man next door. He lets me look at his baseball cards.

We take clothes and toys to the people who live at the shelter in town.

I know my mom and dad love Jesus,
because they take us to church
every week. We go there to worship.

We sing and pray to
Jesus and listen to his
words, just like at home,
only we do it together
with our friends.

They love Jesus too!

Church is **SOOO** much fun!

I like it when Mom and Dad help with my class. They do all kinds of fun things to help us learn about Jesus. We're a good team because we get lots of practice at home!

Jesus must be really special, because he forgives us when we do things that don't make him happy. I know, because I did something **very** bad.

I couldn't help it. I just **had** to have a Choco-Num-Num bar! So I put it in my pocket. But that's stealing.

You know how I said my mom knows all about Jesus' words? Well, she said Jesus wants us not to steal . . . **ever!**

Uh-oh! I knew I had made a bad choice. So, I told her what I did and said I was sorry.

Mom said I had two more things to do. I knew what she meant. I put the candy bar back. Then I asked Jesus to forgive me. Whew! I won't make **that** mistake again!

Mom and Dad make mistakes sometimes too.
But they always say they're sorry.

I remember a time when we were all working
together in the yard. All my leaves blew
away, and Dad just started yelling! I didn't
understand why.

But then Dad told me he was sorry and asked
me to forgive him. He said he felt a little
grumpy because his back was hurting.

My shirt got tears on it
when I hugged him.

Mom and Dad tell me that they will
always love me, and that Jesus loves
me **even** more.

Yep! Jesus must be really special, because
my mom and dad love him **SO** much!

Guess what, Jesus?

I love you too!

Jennie Bishop's experiences bring a refreshing dose of reality to her portrayal of family life in *Jesus Must Be Really Special*. A busy mom herself, Jennie balances family life with an international speaking ministry for PurityWorks, an organization devoted to helping parents teach their children how to embrace purity as a lifestyle. Her best-selling purity parables, *The Princess and the Kiss* and *The Squire and the Scroll*, have been translated into several languages. Jennie and her family live in central Florida. For more information on their ministry, visit www.purityworks.org.

Amy Wummer's whimsical illustrations have appeared in a wide array of children's publications, including books for Random House, Barron's, and Ideals, as well as in magazines such as *Highlights for Children*, *Humpty Dumpty*, *U*S*Kids*, *Ladybug*, *Babybug*, and *Weekly Reader*. In addition to painting, she enjoys cooking and entertaining. Amy and her artist husband, Mark, live in Reading, Pennsylvania, and have three young-adult children.